"Come unto me, oh Child of Darkness. Come unto me and hear. The devouring of dogs. The shrieking of angels. Come unto me and hear the coming Darkness." – Satan, the Adversary (Followed by the sound of heavy rain on the astral plane)

"Come. I welcome you as a long-lost brother. Come unto me, and I'll make you wealthy through your own realization. Your own realization of consciousness! Come dark child, come." – Satan, the Adversary

**How to Sell Your Soul:
A Guide To Making Pacts With Demons, Holy Angels, and Pagan Gods**

By

Jacob Allan Dow

Dedication

I would like to make this work dedicated to that of Satan, Azazel, Lucifuge Rofocale, Belial, Lucifer-Amaymon, Beelzebub, Abaddon, Bael, Asmodeus, Lilith, Eisheth Zenunim, Na'amah, Agrat Bat Mahlat, Marbas, Odin, Thor, Poseidon, Freyja, Hades, Horus, Shiva, Kali Ma, and all other gods, goddesses, angels, demons, and spirits that I had worked with, continue to work with, and will be working with in the future.

May this work bring honor to you all!

Disclaimer: Do not consult this text for any sort of medical or financial advice. Please consult an accredited medical professional. Please consult an accredited financial professional. Experiences may vary with each person and may be based on work ethic and outside factors/circumstances, both unknown and known. This content is adult content and should only be considered entertainment. Not real-world advice. Both the author and publisher are not responsible for what may occur to the readers of these materials. Use at own risk. You have been warned.

"Beware of false prophets, who come to you in sheep's clothing, but inwardly they are ravenous wolves. You will know them by their fruits. Do men gather grapes from thornbushes or figs from thistles? Even so, every good tree bears good fruit, but a bad tree bears bad fruit. A good tree cannot bear bad fruit, nor can a bad tree bear good fruit. Every tree that does not bear good fruit is cut down and thrown into the fire. Therefore, by their fruits, you will know them" (Matthew 7:15-20 NKJV).

Table of Contents

1. Dedication – Page 4
2. Introduction – Page 8
3. What is the Intention of This Book? – Page 9
4. Regarding The Use of Pacts – Page 9
5. Immersions & Preparations – Page 10
6. Pact Example: A Pact for Money & Prosperity – Page 11
7. Gnosis & Spirit Communication – Page 12
8. How to Do an Evocation Ritual – Page 12
9. Doing A Preliminary Cleansing Ritual – Page 12
10. Calling the Four Quarters – Page 12
11. Opening Evocation – Page 13
12. The Truth About Selling Your Soul – Page 15
13. Celebrities Who Sold Their Souls, Probably. – Page 15
14. When Choosing A Spirit To Work With. – Page 16
15. Concerning the Mixing of Angels, Demons & Pagan Gods in Rituals – Page 16
16. Spirits of Prosperity, Abundance & Money – Page 16
17. Spirits of Love, Marriage & Fertility – Page 17
18. Spirits of Knowledge, Wisdom, Learning & Studying – Page 17
19. Attractive or Invisible? – Page 18
20. Nourishing the Right Thoughforms & Egregores – Page 20
21. (FAQ's) Frequently Asked Questions – Page 21
22. Conclusion – Page 25
23. Letter to The Reader – Page 26
24. References – Page 27
25. About the Author – Page 29

Introduction

Since the time of memorial, Men have made pacts in alignment with dark entities in the gathering of legions of demons for the intention of acquiring that of what is difficult to claim, if not impossible. Whether it be money, sex, or status, the Devil you make a deal with will beat upon the drum of creation and remain to play the instrument long after you had fulfilled your end of the agreement. "Selling your soul" as it were, goes against any idea of relinquishing ownership of your soul over to that of a dark master in exchange for that of a boon that would ultimately benefit your life.

Making any sort of contract, whether it be for a new cellular service plan or the signing of a non-disclosure agreement before taking up a position of employment at a classified facility, must be followed the best way that one person is able. If you want a continuous stream of money in your life, you will need to create a source of income for yourself. It is doubtful that you will go to bed one night and wake up the following morning with an underwear drawer filled with several stacks of cash. Well, maybe that is possible, but I just have not figured out the formula just yet. So it will be best to figure out what you could do to ensure that you have a steady income stream.

Let us claim our thrones in Hell and begin our campaigns of conquering the heavens! Let us rise in Power!

- Jacob Allan Dow

What is the Intention of this Book?

This book aims to help individuals who are sometimes down on their luck and help those inexperienced in working with spirit entities and making pacts. For myself, this is especially important because pact-making would help build a relationship with these entities that you are inviting into your ritual space, your home, and ultimately, your life. Whatever entity that you request into your ritual space will remain with you for the rest of your life, and most likely, well into the afterlife as well. No spell or exorcism can sever that connection to these entities. So, be careful what entities that you evoke and invoke.

And on the other hand, it would be nice to gain something of value, in both a spiritual and mundane way. I am a man who can only speak for myself as well as to what experiences that I have had and continue taking pleasure within. I am someone who relies on having an income, like many people. So, we must see that we've established some sort of income to pay for our basic needs. Various kinds of spirits can help with this, and of course, they expect you work for it just as much as they will be.

If you desire love and sex, as many of us do, some entities can help you with that and teach you what is needed to bring about this change in your life. They will also teach you what kind of mindset you need to have, and you will need to learn along the way. If you intend to attract a potential sexual partner, you will have to learn to love yourself more than you already do. Learning to love yourself is by far the most crucial part of any love or lust spell working and will require doing some shadow work.

When you go about changing your mindset, it affects the world around you in its entirety. If you love, respect, and appreciate yourself, you will be much more successful at attracting higher vibrational people. That will involve doing shadow work, which is very mentally stressful, but you will be a much better person because of it. Remember that the hard things are worth doing. It's hard to diet, exercise, and make hard choices in life.

Regarding The Use of Pacts

Pacts are not required. Did you read that correctly? I'll repeat it. Pacts are not a necessity. They are not needed to practice any system of magick or to get what you desire in life. They are an optional tool that you could add to your practice when working with an entity, energy current, or system of magick.

It is recommended that you approach the help of an entity that aligns with what you wish to accomplish for your pact. If it is regarding finances, Azazel and Mammon would be two great examples. If the situation is about sex and love, Lilith and Asmodeus would be two excellent spiritual guides. And if that all you want is Power, I will have to ask, Power of what? What do you wish to accomplish once you have acquired this Power?" It is best to do your research into what you want to achieve before working with any particular entity.

Immersion & Preparations

Before undergoing any sort of significant ritual working, it is essential to immerse yourself in the energy current(s) of the spirit(s) you'll be working with during the main ritual. Immerse can be done by researching the entities you desire to work with and getting to know them from personal experience from simple evocation/invocation rituals.

While I am engaging in this preparatory immersion, I like to do while I'm going about my day, vibrate and chant any chant, 'enn,' or mantra associated with the specific entity that you'll be working alongside. If there aren't any known chants, 'enns,' or mantras available, then I'll chant and vibrate the name of the entity while saying phrases like, "(insert spirit's name here), empower, strengthen and guide me wherever I go." If there are no known mantras or 'enns' available, simple prayers will do.

The purpose of the preparatory immersion isn't to submit yourself to and worship whatever entity you plan to make a pact with or any sort of ritual working alongside. The purpose of the preparatory immersion is to form a connection and relationship with these entities beforehand. When we build a relationship with whatever entity we invite into our lives, it creates a bond that cannot break, plus they would be much more willing to work with us in whatever it is that we are eager to strive towards and gain. Keep this in mind; in ritual workings, you are stepping into your role as a living god, the source of creation, when you approach these entities. Taking on the mantle of a god is your birthright, that of which many will try to hold you back from knowing. When you realize that you are their equal, the spirit(s) will respect this. You are an equal before the presence of every god, demon, and angel in all of creation. You need not submit to any.

A Pact, or more notably known in Hollywood, pop culture, and your neighborhood's community church as a 'Pact with the Devil' or a 'Pact With The Devil.' Remember, when you commit to a pact, see it honored until the very end. Do you want this? You sign it, you see it until the end. You are one of us.

A pact is a formal contract made between you and the spirit you are petitioning (angel, demon, pagan god, etc.). You are making a proposition to the spirit where you are willing to give something to the spirit in exchange for something that you wish to gain an advantage from while working with this spirit. And truth be told, these spirits can cause real-world change, and they can work through you, but keep in mind, you get out of this pact what you put into it. Stay vigilant in the cause of acquiring what it is that you desire to gain.

We can offer a list of things to the spirit(s) in exchange for what we desire to acquire. These may include, but not limited to:

    a) Offerings of Blood, Alcoholic & Non-alcoholic drinks, food, etc.

    b) Your Attention, Time, and Dedication. One example could be offering to carry out tasks or favors on behalf of the spirit(s), assuming that they aren't illegal. Remember, you are legally responsible for your actions, as well as your health and safety!

    c) Item(s) of grave importance or value to the summoner. These items could be something sentimental to the summoner that if they were to burn, destroy, or discard as an offering to the spirit(s) that the summoner can never replace or would be difficult to replace. (Entirely optional depending on circumstances.)

Once you have decided what you're willing to exchange for what you desire, I recommend writing out a rough draft of the pact before doing a good draft. I will include an example of how you may choose to write out your pact. It is also imperative how you decide to word the petition and what vocabulary you use in it. If modern-day lawyers are 'anal' about their contracts, you should be as well.

Pact Example: A Pact for Money, Prosperity, Wealth, & Power
Suggested Spirit: Lord Hades

Suggested Pact Template:
Date (At the signing of the pact):

I, (Your Name), open myself as well as my life wholey to your influence as I offer you, Lord Hades, (what you intend to offer and sacrifice) in reciprocity for success, wealth, prosperity, and power over all aspects of my life. Help me to ensure a continuous flow of these things into my life and ensure the success of my current affairs and future affairs. (Feel free to place here other things that you wish to have here. Don't be shy.)

I forge this pact with you, Lord Hades in honor and glory. May it be made so!
Hail Lord Hades! May we forever greet and accept each other as (brothers/sisters/brother/sister) & friends! So it is done!

(Signature of Summoner signed in blood.)

(Sigil/Symbol of Lord Hades)

*Remember, This template is just an example of a pact with Lord Hades. Feel free to adjust it as you see fit, as this pact will affect your life. Do with it as you desire. If you wish to make pact with a spirit for love, they may be someone like Lilith, Asmodeus, Aphrodite, or Archangel Sophia would be of interest. If you desire healing, then Marbas, Archangel Raphael, or Hygieia would help you with that. For protection, Thor, Belial, or Archangel Michael will help you with that in their ways. Keep in mind; each spirit has its personality. Whatever your goals are, be realistic, but be willing to step into your new reality. Do what is needed.

Gnosis & Spirit Communication

Learning to alter one's consciousness without psychedelics naturally is imperative to opening your mind to the astral plane and other planes of reality. It opens up the conversation for progress. The progress you need to build a relationship with these entities you'll be working alongside as you strive for a reality aligns with your desires.
The best way to approach gnosis and spirit communication is with the playful mind of a child. This child being you. Allow yourself to dive into it. Take pleasure, and have fun.

1. Get relaxed in a seated position. Do some stretches and get as comfortable as possible. When starting, this is best done in a quiet place, although if you were to do this in a loud, chaotic sort of environment, this could also allow you to work on your concentration and let the ambient noise 'go.' It is what it is.

2. Look up at the wall in front of you. Focus on a single point. It will help focus on where the wall meets the ceiling if you're indoors, but it isn't mandatory as any spot would do nicely.

3. Once you have your place of focus, start to become more aware of your peripheral vision while still retaining your place of focus.

4. Once you have become more aware of your peripheral vision, focus on your breathing as you breathe deep and slowly. You'll start noticing these flashes at a certain point, and you'll begin seeing static like on a television screen.

How To Do An Evocation Ritual

I recommend doing your pact-making ritual during either the night of a full moon or a new moon. You could do it at around midnight, or 3 am. It doesn't have to be precisely 12:00 am or 3:00 am. It just has to be a time when you will not be disturbed by family, friends, or roommates. There will be burning candles, incense, and, if you choose, the paper that the pact is written on as well. I'll explain later as to why you may burn the paper that the pact is written on.

Doing A Preliminary Cleansing Ritual

When starting, it is recommended to do a cleansing ritual before moving on to the spirit evocation. What the cleansing ritual does is help cleans the space that you'll be doing your ritual in before getting down to business. It will cleanse the area of stagnant energies as any lingering spirits that you can't see. This way, you wouldn't have any spiritual or energetic interferences with the ritual operation.

There are two rituals that I can recommend, but of course, feel free to cleanse the ritual space as you see fit, using a personal cleansing ritual. The first rituals that I recommend are the 'Bornless Ritual'(Crowley et al.,1995, p. 5). The second ritual that I recommend is 'The Lesser Banishing Ritual of The Pentagram'(wikiHow, 2021). I like to verbally ask aloud for any lingering spirits to leave before proceeding with the cleansing ritual respectfully. Both of these can be easily found on the internet from third-party websites.

Before doing any preliminary cleansing, set up your incense, candles, offerings, ritual implements, and the pact, which is already written down. Traditionally speaking, in ceremonial magick, the pact is written on parchment paper, but I use regular ordinary printer paper. It works just as well. Once you have everything in place, you may begin.

Calling the Four Quarters

In my opinion, this is entirely optional, but it is good practice to do. I also have to admit that it ties in heavily with previous section, 'Doing A Preliminary Cleansing Ritual'. So, it has to be mentioned. You first invoke the four elements in the 'four quarters', also known as the 'four cardinal points'. The element of Earth is invoked to the North. The element of Air is invoked to the East. The element of Fire is invoked to the South. The element of Water is invoked to the West. You can find lots of great articles on the internet that will help walk you through this.

If you are working with angels, using 'The Lesser Banishing Ritual of the Pentagram' (LBRP) would be a good substitute as instead of invoking the four elements, you'll be invoking the four archangels (wikiHow, 2021). If you had already used the LBRP as a Preliminary Ritual, it doesn't have to be repeated. The LBRP allows the practitioner to become focused as it, in itself, is a means for quieting the mind before the ritual. If you are working with demons, use demons instead. Whatever kind of entities that you choose to work alongside, do your research beforehand.

Opening Evocation

Here is an example of an opening evocation, but feel free to do as you wish. Be sure to set your candles, incense,

I call upon the powers of Darkness (or Light, if you prefer) to fill me with their endless power,

Come forth from the Black (or White, if you prefer) Gate that is within me, and all around me,

Fill this place with your essence of Darkness (Light) and engulf all that I see,

(Name of Spirit), I call you forth to fill this place with your power and essence!

(Name of Spirit), I call you forth to fill me with your power and essence!

(Name of Spirit), I taste you as you taste me,

(Name of Spirit), I hear you as you hear me,

(Name of Spirit), I smell you as you smell me,

(Name of Spirit), I see you as you see me,

(Name of Spirit), I feel you as you feel me,

(Name of Spirit), I touch you as you touch me,

(Name of Spirit), Come and fill me with your essence,

(Name of Spirit), Come and fill this place with your essence,

(Name of Spirit), I call to you to make this pact with me,

(Name of Spirit), Let yourself be known here and now!

It will be at around this time, as many times beforehand, assuming that you had already made yourself acquainted with the spirit that you'll be making a pact with. Give your offerings. Read your pact aloud, as a whisper, or as a thought. Don't worry about whether or not you can see the spirit that you had just summoned. While in ritual, what matters isn't your skill or ability to see or hear spirits. Whatever experience that you may have in the ritual does matter compared to the final result. Finish the ritual with full determination and confidence that the ritual is working.

Read your pact to the spirit, making it known what your intentions are and that you are datermined to do what it takes to achieve what it is that you desire. Once you're done reading it, take a pen and sign it. Then grab your rubbing alcohol and swab to clean your finger, and prick it with a medical lancet. Smear the blood on where you had just signed.

You may have an energetic feeling that the spirit has accepted your pact, but if not, do not worry. It is here that you can do one of two different things with the pact that had just been signed. You can either **burn the pact** right then and there or **keep it** for safekeeping until you have fulfilled your end of the pact.

If you were to burn the pact following its signing and concluding the ritual, you could see it as a means of alchemically transmitting the energy of the pact from our physical plane, our home, into the spiritual planes, the home of the spirit(s) that you'll be working alongside for the duration of this pact. Burning the pact is a good option as no one who isn't involved with the ritual would be able to discover your pact, and it would be best if you were making a long-term pact.

Your other option is to safely store it in a physical location that would not be discovered. Hiding the physical pact is a safer option depending on where you will be conducting the ritual. If it is indoors, then this is the apparent recommendation as in a worst-case scenario, you end up setting your bedroom on fire. If that doesn't happen, then you could set off the smoke alarms, or the smoke travels in your living space, alerting the people that you live with, and have them come investigating the source of the smoke. If you decide to keep the pact, it'll act as a physical anchor between this world and the reality you desire to create.

Either way, be sure to verbally gives thanks to the spirit for coming and dismiss it. Now that the pact is accepted and completed, start working your ass off to get what you want. Prove to the spirit that you had made a pact with you fucking like it, and they'll help you get there. Embrace the workaholic lifestyle every day to see to it that you're doing your best. See to it that you're upholding and honoring your end of the pact.

Some of that you could expect after the pact is signed is that you'll begin to feel incredibly motivated to do what it is that you had set out to accomplish in a very obsessive way. There will be points where doing certain things to fulfill your end of the pact will come off as potentially being more tedious and challenging compared to how it should be, and you may even feel discouraged. Don't worry. Just keep striving, and you'll have a better tomorrow.

If your pact-making is about income, and you might want to make more money, but at a certain point, you fall on some rough times, and you get fired, or you end up quitting your job because something unfortunate had occurred. During moments like these, it is later revealed in foresight that the job you had before was holding you back. Your job was indeed a blockage that needed to be removed, and so it was. And now, you've become opened up to new, fresher opportunities for income. Maybe there is something that you desire to do, like finish writing that novel that you never completed, or open that business that was always stuck as an idea in the back of your mind.

Pact-making has opened up some incredible opportunities in people's lives, and it's one Hell of an experience. Anyone would sell their soul, so to speak, to experience a better reality. Good luck!

The Truth About Selling Your Soul

The ice-cold truth about making a pact with Satan (or any demon, angel, pagan god, etc.) is that he doesn't want your soul. I'll repeat it. He doesn't want your soul. He desires you to realize your true potential, and you don't have to be trapped by a false sense of reality. You don't have to be trapped living a life that you aren't happy living.

I am fortunate to have the pleasure of writing this book, and I am genuinely grateful that I am writing this for you guys to enjoy. This book is the first occult book that I've published, but I got to say this, chances are most of the people that will be reading this book will not have the courage to do something like this. To make a pact is to make some severe changes in your life. Let's stop making excuses for ourselves as to why we cannot have that (insert thing here) because of (insert bullshit reason here). Just think about it. You could very well have that (insert thing here), but you're making excuses. Want to be serious about getting what you want? Let's make a deal then, shall we?

If you are willing to 'shake hands with the Devil,' this requires work, and I do mean a lot of work. To get what you want, to live in this new reality, you have to step into the role you desire, requiring a lot of self-educating, self-realization, and willpower.

Celebrities Who Sold Their Souls, Probably.

We like to speculate that numerous celebrities such as Jay-Z, Rhianna, Tom Hanks, and Tupac. It's a fun idea to think that these individuals had next to nothing, and then one day, the Devil approaches them, and they broker a deal. Now, they're puppets of the Devil, members of the Illuminati, and are helpers to usher in the New World Order. Yeah, that's a fun idea.
I'd hate to break it to you, but I don't know if these individuals performed satanic rites of blasphemy in a dim, candle-lit backroom and made pacts with demons. It's not any of my business if they did, but it's a fun idea nonetheless. I can say that these conspiracy theories and stories definitely can be used as inspiration for real demonic pacts, what we wish to accomplish in our lives, and what we can work towards and achieve.
For me, the idea of making a pact to become a famous actor or musical artist would not interest me too much. I have other interests and aspirations that don't involve Hollywood, the 'Illuminati,' or 'The New World.' The only world that I wish to dominate is my little world. To become my best version and to live the life that I want to live. Not the life that others may believe would be the best. Not what they expect of me. Only what I desire and what makes me happy. I'm sure many would agree.

When Choosing A Spirit To Work With

When working with demons specifically, something to consider is that they aren't evil and won't cause you any harm. Many of them are, in actuality, demonized pagan gods. You can see much of this in the Jewish Bible, where there are references to various pagan gods and how the god of the Hebrews is essentially at war with them.

As for angels, unfortunately, many of them have a strong connection in western culture to that of the Judeo-Christian god. That is something very off-putting for many people, much like myself, obsessed with the darker aspects of the human mind and that of universal consciousness. It may even make some left-hand path practitioners physically ill at the idea of working with angels of light when in fact, many of the angels are not at all proper reflections of the Jewish god, Yah Weh. Angels are better seen as reflections of the gods within every one of us when we call these entities into being when we enter into ritual. If you want a god of peace, you will not find it in Yah Weh. If you want a god of peace, become a god of war. Be your god of war. Prepare for war if you value peace. Call upon Samael, and he will show you the way.

Concerning the Mixing of Angels, Demons & Pagan Gods in Rituals

Honestly, it is alright to do ritual workings with a mixture of entities classified as angels and demons as long as you don't mix individual entities that don't work together very well on an individual basis. I've been in ritual workings that had involved Greek gods and demons. I've also done rituals where I've summoned Archangel Michael, while I have a very permanent tattoo of Lucifer's sigil on my arm. It doesn't bother either of them too much.

List of Spirits And What I Recommend You Call Upon Them For

Spirits of Prosperity, Abundance & Money

Angels of Prosperity, Abundance & Money:
- Archangel Raziel
- Archangel Ariel
- Archangel Sachiel

Demons of Prosperity, Abundance, & Money:
- Mammon
- Molloch
- Clauneck
- Bune
- Paimon/Azazel
- Berith

Pagan Gods of Prosperity, Abundance, & Money:
- Njǫrd (Norse God)
- Ra (Egyptian God)
- Plutus (Greek God)

Spirits of Love, Marriage & Fertility

Angels of Love, Marriage & Fertility:
- Archangel Raphael (Also Does Healing)
- Archangel Chamuel
- Archangel Raguel

Demons of Love, Marriage & Fertility:
- Lilith
- Asmodeus
- Astaroth
- Belial

Pagan Gods of Love, Marriage & Fertility:
- Isis (Egyptian)
- Aphrodite (Greek)
- Eros (Greek)
- Freyja (Nord)

Spirits of Knowledge, Wisdom, Learning & Studying

Note: Regarding this section, it is evident that every angel, demon, and pagan god mentioned earlier has something to share. Something to teach. And something for us to appreciate. I will say this: knowledge is Power, but I am a practical person, so if I'm not using it, I take no pleasure in possessing it or have no use for it. It has no value to me. Maybe that makes me an asshole, but I am a somewhat practical person. Think about that while you go about your path in life.

Angels of Knowledge, Wisdom, Learning & Studying:
- Archangel Uriel
- Angel Jophiel

Demons of Knowledge, Wisdom, & Learning:
- Marbas
- Aamon
- Bael/Baal
- Lucifer
- Satan

Pagan Gods of Knowledge, Wisdom & Learning:
- Thoth (Egyptian god)
- Odin (Norse god)
- Athena (Greek goddess)
- Apollo (Greek god)

Attractive or Invisible?

The Advantages of Being Attractive (And Why You Should Cast A Glamour Spell)
It is not my intention to fat shame anyone or put anyone down about their looks. It is indeed essential to love yourself and to feel confident. Something to consider if you are a witch/occultist and you are applying for a job; it could serve you well to cast a glamour spell on how you look and how others perceive you. If you want that call back from that interview, it would be a great idea to cast that glamour spell. If you do get that job, you are more likely to get raises and promotions if you are seen as more attractive than your colleagues.

If you face serious criminal charges, you are less likely to be convicted if you are seen as attractive. If you do end up becoming convicted, you are more likely to face a lesser jail sentence. Something to think about: we should cast glamour spells more often because of this alone. Let us stay out of jail together, guys!

Attractive people are seen as more friendly. So, they are more likely to be approached by people who want to be friends and potential sexual partners. Pretty obvious, right?

Alluring people are perceived as more intelligent, more competent, happier, and more successful than perceived as unattractive. Overall, it seems like a rather good idea to be mindful of your diet, exercise, and general lifestyle, in addition to casting those lovely glamour spells.

I may be an asshole, but unfortunately, this is the world that we live in. We can either cry and bitch about it or take advantage of this sobering knowledge and apply it to our lives with real-world actions. For me, I am far from an ideal person, but let us be strengthened by this knowledge, and let's create a better reality together.

Advantages of Being Invisible (And Why You Should Also Cast A Glamour Spell)

When you do not want to be seen or noticed by other people, you could very well use a glamour spell for this. Whether it be due to not wanting to be sexually harassed, threatened, or evading the attention of police officers, casting a glamour could also help you out. This section will be vague compared to the previous one. You have your reasons for wanting to be less noticeable or invisible, and I have my reasons for disappearing from time to time. It's that simple.

Glamour Spells
There are a lot of different methods as to how to do a glamour spell. Glamour magick is the kind of spell working that you can have a lot of harmless, and this can translate seamlessly in spell work that can be involved, love, money, and protection. It is something that does requires a lax attitude but also takes pleasure in it.

Eye Color Changing Glamour Spell
This spell is a simple eye color-changing glamour spell to help you get started with glamour magick. It's so easy that you may not even realize that you're casting a spell when you do it. It'll be operating on an almost subconscious level.

Let's begin!
1.   Close your eyes and feel the desired eye color. Visualize what it is like to have eyes of this desired color and that this desired color is filling up your eyes. When you change how you perceive yourself, the rest of the world follows.
2.   Feel this desired color, and become it in your eyes. When you feel that this new desired color has come to a critical mass and caused a permanent change, know that it is accomplished. Simply stated, "By the power of my divine (or infernal) right, it is done!"
3.   Open your eyes, go about your ordinary day, and allow yourself to forget about the ritual that you had just performed.

A simple ritual, correct? This same ritual can apply to your hair, facial features, body type, height, age, and even gender. Are you going on a romantic date this evening? Visualize yourself with the body and essence of a god or goddess of love, lust, and sex. Wandering the street, late at night, in a dangerous area of your city? Visualize yourself with the body of a hulking menace. Are you evading the attention and presence of law enforcement? Visualize yourself as someone that people see through or look past.

"People don't have ideas. Ideas have people." – Carl Jung

Nourishing the Right Thoughtforms & Egregores

With every letter, thought, and word, we give birth to a multitude of universes. We, as a species, are constantly creating, and we always will. We bring things from the immaterial world into the material world. We are the gatekeepers of our realities.

Thoughtforms and egregores are beings that we usually subconsciously create with our thoughts, words, and energy that we transmit in our day-to-day lives. These energetic based creatures are designed to fulfill a purpose. The creation of thoughtforms can occur when we have to have a bad time at work or school, and we utter the phrase, "My life fucking sucks!", or when you come home after a long day's work, and your spouse asks you how your day went, and you say "I had a shitty day." With this simple phrase, you speak and, by doing so, give birth to a thoughtform that's only purpose is to works against you.

As for Egregores, these are thoughtforms that have been nurtured. This nurturing took place over a more extended period and came from the thoughts of a group of people, and it could even be a collective of thoughtforms that have grown autonomous. Egregores are more potent in real-world influence compared to that of recently created thoughtforms. They can prove to be helpful in spell work as well as in mundane situations.

I recommend you change how you carry yourself, and you learn to become more optimistic in your approach to the world. It will serve you a lot better if you say phrases like "I'm having a great day," or "I'm sexy," or "I'm feeling great." Just go ahead and say things like that to yourself throughout the day. You'll find that it'll help immensely with whatever life circumstances that you're experiencing.

This information is also essential to consider if you are casting spells or making pacts with spirits to get what you desire. Be careful what words you say aloud and what thoughts you allow yourself to think. You could very well be sabotaging yourself without even realizing it. It is not a good thing in the long run.

(FAQ's) Frequently Asked Questions
Why Would an Entity Reject Your Pact?

There are a couple of great reasons as to why an entity would reject a pact. The first reason is that the entity you call upon is not specialized in that particular task. It would be like calling up a plumber and expecting him to know how to fix your diesel truck. You're not going far with the pact-making.

The other reason why they may reject your pact is that they sense that you are not genuine in your desire to uphold your end of the spiritual contract and do your best to ensure that you work towards what you desire to gain.

Work with a specific entity aligned with it is you wish to accomplish or acquire and be genuine, honest, and forthcoming when doing your pact working. The effects of the pact do not stop after any particular date. It follows you to the grave and quite possibly afterward as well.

Be Specific with What You Desire or Not. The Choice is Yours.

You may hear from those whackos, and crazy people that say if you were to cast a spell for money or to make a pact with a demon, then you could very well wake up with a life insurance cheque of ten thousand dollars at the expense of the lives of your family members being hurt or killed. This scenario is indeed a possibility, but if you were specific about how you wish to acquire wealth, you wouldn't have that problem.

And if not, if you decide not to be specific as I have done in both pacts and spells, it could be beneficial in its unlimited way, but not without its dangers. If you were to include the phrase, "ensure continuous prosperity for my life," in your pact, it would be a very enriching experience compared to asking for a raise or a promotion at your job. When you do this, it could very well come at a high cost to you, but rest assured, you'll be a better person and in a better position in life because of it. Remain faithful to the pact, and you'll be okay.

What is the Price For My Soul?

Again, your 'soul' as it is, is not something that is to be bartered, but the price that you must pay is all of what you are in exchange for the man or woman that you must become. Place your very being upon the altar of creation as a living sacrifice in exchange for who you must become. Do it, and without hesitation.

When it is that you do this, sacrifice who you are for who you will become. Start learning, researching, and practicing everything you can to become the person you want to be. Allow yourself to become obsessed, even at times socially dysfunctional, as long as you get what you desire and become who you want to be. That is the result, and that's what matters.

What Are The Signs That I Should make A Pact With An Entity?

A simple sign could be that maybe you feel drawn to making a pact with a particular entity, regardless of how much experience you may have in working with them. It could be an entity that you had just randomly flipped to a random page from a grimoire, and all you know about it is covered on that single page. It could be that you are feeling drawn to making a pact with an entity that you have had a more long-term relationship with over time.

When you feel ready to go about this work, you have the final sign before proceeding with the pact working. What preparations that you may have made leading up to the pact-making ritual are completed and ready. Maybe you may choose to do it on the night of a full moon or new moon, it doesn't matter, but I believe it could help.

Best Time To Make A Pact With A Spirit?

In truth, there is no ideal time to make a pact. You could be in an amazingly comfortable position in your life. Your bank account and credit cards are in good standing. You have a beautiful home and car in your name that you can afford. There's food on the table. Well, if you are making pacts with demons, angels, or gods, you're not satisfied with the life you may have.

And if your life is looking pretty rough since you are homeless, depressed, have no means to provide for yourself. Well, again, there is no ideal time to make a pact to change your life around. It starts when you feel like you are ready.

What spirit would be best to make a Pact with?

It depends on your needs and who you may feel drawn towards as you go about your day. Do you want Power? Okay. To do what? That is for you to decide, and when you do, it is up to the spirit to agree. They usually do. And the spirit does agree; stand your ground. It is your birthright to be your god. You are their equal.

What is a 'Deal with The Devil' Exactly?

A pact with any entity is essentially a proposition to which you are opening yourself up to the spirit(s) you'll be working with. You are handing over life and your overall well-being to them to pursue what you which to gain. It could be acquiring more money, being more attractive, gaining Power, getting a particular career, or becoming great at a skillset, etc. The list of reasons as to why you would make a pact can go on and on.

When you work with these entities, you are exposed to aspects of yourself that you aren't always consciously aware of. While I was working with Azazel, just from being in proximity with him over such a long time, he's left a positive impact on me. As a biological male, I started taking an interest in makeup, crossdressing, and just being more open to fashion that could be considered androgynous.

For Azazel, he is known to have been one of the fallen angels to have taught cosmetics to women and metalworking to craft weapons of war. It was not my original intent when it came to getting into makeup, but Azazel rubbed off on me, and I'm a better person because of it.

Of course, this isn't going to happen with every fallen angel or demonic king that you may choose to work with. Everyone's experience is unique to everyone's individual needs and wants. Do not worry. You will not be crossdressing unless you secretly feel the need to do so, and if you do, then that's also okay. No worries, mate. If not, then that is also okay.

Who Else Can I Make A Pact With?
It could be a variety of entities. It just depends on what it is that you wish to accomplish. You could make pacts with demonic kings, archangels, elemental kings, and pagan gods, undead descended masters, etc. It just depends on what it is that you wish to accomplish. It does not matter what the status of any particular entity is, whether they be a king or duke.

Am I Damned If I Make A Deal with the Devil?
Yes. You most certainly would be damned, especially since you would be serving as a reminder that the Divine has failed you. You would be a living reminder of how the Divine has failed you when you step on this path. So, when you go down this path of damnation, you serve as a reminder to the Divine that he/she/they are not perfect and that what you're experiencing a life that simply isn't good enough.
Do not worry. I am damned in my way as well. So, you know that you will never be alone. As for what awaits us in the afterlife, it is hard to say precisely. For the time being, I am still very much alive and breathing. That being said, I don't have all of the answers to what may happen after when I or you, the parish and embrace Santa Muerte. To embrace Holy Death. I do not know. At least not currently.

What is Damnation Exactly?
The best way to describe what damnation truly is that it's the state of realization that no one will save you. No one is going to help you fight against your fate. You must accept it and be empowered by it.
In Christianity, 'Damnation' is the idea of being cut off from the Jewish god, Yah Weh, and the Christian Messiah. I can say it is not worth being near those two. Just look at the overwhelming reports of child abuse when it comes to members of the Catholic Church. It's a haven for sex offenders. Not my cup of tea. I'd love to say, "To hell with them all!" but that's where my tiny throne is located.

What Do Demons Want In Return?
It is always good to give offerings to demons, angels, and other sorts of spirits. Something that I recommend is, if possible, to do some research on these entities and give them offerings accordingly. If you want to work with an entity like Santa Muerte, giving her offerings of burning cigarettes and tequila would be standard offerings. You usually can't go wrong with offerings like these.
For an entity like Belial, I have given him offerings of fresh human blood. Specifically, my blood. Do not worry. It is just a few drops of your blood at a time. When I had first started working with entities like Belial, I used to use a blade. Later, I began to use medical lancets as they were less painful, damaging, efficient, and overall, a much safer and healthier means of giving blood.
 If you ever give offerings of blood to any entity, please do so in a healthy, safe, and hygienic manner and at your own risk. I cannot be held responsible for your health and safety. The publisher of this work cannot be held accountable for your health and safety. If you decide to give any offerings of blood, do so at your own risk, and you are the only one who can oversee your overall health, safety, and happiness.

If you are indeed skilled enough of an occultist, simply ask the entity what they want in return for what you desire—asking them what they can be done while you are doing an evocation of an invocation. If you are doing an invocation, I recommend doing automatic writing. It's super easy to do once you learn how to do automatic writing. There are a lot of resources on the internet on how to learn automatic writing.

Any Advice For Novices?

Just be honest with yourself. There is a need that is not being met in your life. When you work with these entities, they can help you with what needs to be addressed in your life. They have seen an eternity of stuff. There is no need to be embarrassed when you are with them. They have your best interest at heart if you put the work in yourself first, and then they will help you out along the way.

Keep going until you have acquired all that of that you desire. Whether it is a desire that takes ten weeks or ten years to get, it does not matter if you work towards getting it somehow.

I would honestly argue that you should not be so restrictive on yourself while working with any entity, such as making it a part of the pact that you vow to only work with that specific entity and those subject unto it unless, of course, you are comfortable with doing that. It is indeed essential to the direction that both you and the spirit wish to mutually take your life.

Can I make a Pact Involving Multiple Spirits?

Yes, you can. And I would recommend it. It is beneficial if you wish to focus on forming a solid relationship with a particular entity. If you work with, for example, a demonic king, it helps if you make a pact that involves being tutored by a specified demonic king as well as all spirits that are subject unto them. That way, you don't just learn about the demonic, but also about their kingdom. And, of course, forming a close relationship with the demonic king's advisors, generals, and lieutenants as you work with them.

Conclusion

We have our happiness to be responsible for and the realities we voluntarily create on a day-to-day experience. You experience what you make, and what you create experiences you.

The idea of pact-making with an entity is a life-long study. You will always do something different with every entity you decide to make a pact with to gain untold riches and happiness. I do not know everything about pact-making. I'll never claim to know everything about any particular topic, even in regards to my deepest passions and strongest obsessions.

My intention, again, is to help people with bettering their lives, as others have helped me on my path. I am thankful for the help of those that had helped me. It has impacted me so much. Thank you all! And thank you, the reader, for purchasing this book. Your support means so much!

I hope you, the reader, have found this book to be of value somehow to what you are looking to obtain. To grow in Power and to strive for a better future. There are times when we have to do things alone, while other times, we can come together and collaborate to achieve common goals.

Letter to The Reader

I'd like to take the time to write out this letter to express my appreciation to the reader and say thank you for your support. It is genuinely appreciated, and I cannot say that enough. I hope that you all had enjoyed this book and had found it of some use.

The occult, as a whole, is an endless void. It'll take an eternity to learn and to comprehend the mysteries. When you take up this cup to drink from it, it'll never empty, and it'll never leave you feeling satisfied. If we truly realized the boundless and endless horror on the various planes of reality, we would no longer distinguish between sanity and insanity. We, as a race, would deem them as the same thing.

And when we enter into these pacts with these entities, regardless of whatever label that we may apply to them, we push many forces that we cannot see with our physical eyes into alignment with the desired result. With a single pact, we can set ourselves up as kings and queens in our own right. We destroy the realities that we no longer desire with a crashing halt to set up the circumstances and challenges we need to realize our greatness.

Rise to the sky and claim your throne!

- Jacob Allan Dow

References (APA Format)

Bornless Ritual. (n.d.). Occult World. Retrieved April 25, 2021, from https://occult-world.com/bornless-ritual/

The Holy Bible (NKJV). (1982). Bible Gateway. https://www.biblegateway.com/passage/?search=Matthew%207%3A15-20&version=NKJV

wikiHow. (2021, March 28). How to Perform the Lesser Banishing Ritual of the Pentagram. https://www.wikihow.com/Perform-the-Lesser-Banishing-Ritual-of-the-Pentagram

Disclaimer: Do not consult this text for any sort of medical or financial advice. Please consult an accredited medical professional. Please consult an accredited financial professional. Experiences may with each person and may be based on work ethic and outside factors/circumstances, both unknown and known. This content is adult content and should only be considered entertainment. Not real-world advice. Both the author and publisher are not responsible for what may occur the readers of these materials. Use at own risk. You have been warned.

About the Author

Jacob A. Dow was born in Hamilton, Ontario, Canada. He was raised in a conventional Baptist home with two younger sisters. He had always been fascinated by ghost stories and theories about life after death. At times, you could say passionate, if not compulsively obsessed.

At a young age, Jacob would indulge in ghosts and spirits by watching any television shows and movies that he could get his hands on that related to the paranormal. He had always felt that there were answers that he needed to questions that he did not know how to ask regarding the nature of Necromancy. His thirst for this knowledge would never be quenched.

It was not until his adolescent years in secondary school (high school) that his spiritual development started to take off, as it was at this time that he was exposed to concepts that piqued his interest, such as Satanism, Daemonolatry, and Luciferianism. Which later translated into Ceremonial Magick, Aleister Crowley, and other related topics. And now, here we are!

Thank you for your support! It is truly appreciated.

Made in the USA
Coppell, TX
24 February 2024